Taco Soup Cookbook

Plunge Into the Irresistible Taste of Taco Soup

BY

Jayden Dixon

JAYDEN DIXON

Copyright Notes

Fortunately, all of my readers are really nice people, and I don't have to worry too much about asking everyone to please refrain from sharing my work with others because then I don't get credit for it. Either way, I still like to add a little section in all of my books specifying what is NOT allowed so you can avoid copyright infringements.

Do not sell, re-publish, distribute, or make any print or electronic reproductions of this book in parts or as a whole unless you have express written consent from my team or me. We're so strict about it because we value our work and want to receive proper credit for all the time we put into this book.

Anyway, I know this isn't going to be an issue...I just had to put it out there just in case. With that out of the way, we can finally start cooking, so let's go!

Table of Contents

Introduction

Taco soup first ever originated in the Southern part of the United States back in the 1950s. so, you can imagine people have come a long way to love taco soup as it has its popularity even today. Now people around the world make it in their kitchens with ease. Some people who never tried this recipe at home may find it rather difficult as it feels like a lot of ingredients and a lot of time when you are enjoying it in a restaurant. But the truth of the matter is, you can simplify it at home.

The basic ingredients of taco soup are green chilies, tomatoes, onion, taco seasoning, choice of meat, beans, and corn. But the fun thing about making anything in the kitchen is you can spice things up according to your choice. You can make it without corn. You can make it with any tomatoes. You can make it with beef, chicken, turkey, lamb, mutton, or pork. You can also make it vegetarian with no meat at all. You can make it with kidney beans, lima beans, navy beans, chickpeas, or lentils. You can make it without beans too. So the choice is yours how you want to make it.

The time it may take to prepare a taco soup depends on your choice of ingredients and your choice of utensils. Try all the 30 recipes and see which taco soup you love most.

1. Lamb Taco Soup

Taco soup itself is delicious. When you add a protein like lamb to it, the flavors get uplifted by dozen times.

Preparation Time: 10 minutes

Cooking Time: 6 hours

Serves: 6

Ingredients:

- 2 lb. Lamb, boneless, cut into small cubes
- 1 cup corn kernels
- 1 can (14oz) stewed tomatoes
- 1 can (14oz) kidney beans
- 1 can (14oz) lima beans
- 1 cup avocado, cubed
- 1 cup cheddar cheese, grated
- 1/2 cup tomatoes, chopped
- 6 tbsp sour cream
- 2 tbsp cilantro, chopped
- 1 tsp garlic powder
- Salt and pepper
- 4 cups vegetable broth
- 1/3 cup taco seasoning

Instructions:

Drain the beans. In a slow cooker, add the beans.

Add the lamb, and vegetable broth.

Cover and cook for 4 hours.

Add the stewed tomatoes, corn kernels, seasoning, and spices, and cook for 2 hours.

Add cilantro, cheese, avocado, tomatoes, and sour cream on top before serving.

2. Beef Taco Soup

The beef taco soup is wholesome and easy. It is a simple one-pot dish.

Preparation Time: 20 minutes

Cooking Time: 4 hours

Serves: 8

Ingredients:

- 2 lb. ground beef
- 1 cup corn kernels
- 2 can (28oz) stewed tomatoes
- 2 cans (28oz) lima beans
- 1 cup tomatoes, chopped
- 2 tbsp cilantro, chopped
- 1 tsp onion powder
- 1 tsp garlic powder
- Salt and pepper
- 4 cups vegetable broth
- 1/2 cup taco seasoning

Instructions:

In a crockpot, add ground beef, and vegetable broth.

Add tomatoes, stewed tomatoes, corn, lime bean, spices, and seasoning.

Cover with a lid and cook for 4 hours.

Add cilantro and serve hot.

3. Spicy Beef Taco Soup

The delicious taco soup with tomatoes, corn, beef, and kidney beans is amazing with all spices like paprika, cumin, garlic, etc.

Preparation Time: 10 minutes

Cooking Time: 1 hour

Serves: 4

Ingredients:

- 1 cup minced beef
- 1 cup corn kernels
- 1 cup crushed tomatoes
- 1 can (14oz) kidney beans
- 2 tomatoes, chopped
- 1 tsp garlic
- 1 tsp onion powder
- 1 tsp paprika
- 1 tsp cumin
- 2 tbsp taco seasoning
- Salt and pepper

Instructions:

In a pressure cooker, add the minced beef.

Add the crushed tomatoes.

Add 4 cups of water. Add salt, pepper, taco seasoning, cumin, paprika, onion, garlic, and kidney beans.

Add the chopped tomatoes and corn kernels.

Cover with a lid and cook for 1 hour on medium-high heat.

Serve hot.

4. Quick Creamy Beef Taco Soup

The creaminess of this soup is what everyone loves the most. The topping like cheese, crispy tortillas, and avocado, also adds up to making the soup irresistible.

Preparation Time: 5 minutes

Cooking Time: 2 hours

Serves: 6

Ingredients:

- 1 1/2 cups minced beef
- 1 cup corn kernels
- 1 cup crushed tomatoes
- 1 can (140z) coconut milk
- 1 can (14oz) kidney beans, drained
- 2 tomatoes, chopped
- 1 tsp garlic
- 1 tsp paprika
- 2 tbsp taco seasoning
- Salt and pepper
- Cilantro, chopped to serve
- Avocado cubes to serve
- Tortillas chips, crushed, to serve
- Cheddar cheese, grated, to serve

Instructions:

In a large pot, add the beef and sauté for 3 minutes.

Add the crushed tomatoes, coconut milk, and spices.

Cook for 2 minutes. Pour in 4 cups of water. Cover and cook for 40 minutes.

Add corn, kidney beans, and tomatoes.

Add seasoning and cook for 20 minutes.

Serve with avocado, tortilla chips, cheddar, and cilantro on top. Add parchment paper to a baking sheet.

5. Spicy Bean Lamb Taco Soup

The spices in the recipe do all the magic for this soup recipe. If you are a spice lover then you have to fall in love with this taco soup.

Preparation Time: 10 minutes

Cooking Time: 2 hours

Serves: 8

Ingredients:

- 2 cups minced lamb
- 1 cup corn kernels
- 2 can (28oz) lima beans, drained
- 1 cup crushed tomatoes
- 2 tomatoes, chopped
- 1 tsp garlic
- 1 tbsp red chili powder
- 1 can (14oz) black beans, drained
- 1 tsp onion powder
- 2 tbsp taco seasoning
- 2 tsp paprika
- Salt and pepper
- Cilantro, chopped to serve

Instructions:

Take a pressure cooker, and sauté the lamb for 4 minutes.

Add the crushed tomatoes, spices, and beans.

Cook for 20 minutes. Pour in 6 cups of water.

Add the spices and seasoning and cook for 1 hour.

Add the corn kernels, and tomatoes and cook for 20 minutes.

Take off the heat. Serve with cilantro on top.

6. Chicken Cheesy and Creamy Taco Soup

The cheesiness and creaminess of this soup are amazing.

Preparation Time: 10 minutes

Cooking Time: 1 hour

Serves: 6

Ingredients:

- 1 cup minced chicken
- 1 cup jalapeno, chopped
- 1 cup corn kernels
- 2 tbsp taco seasoning
- 1 cup cheddar, grated
- 2 cups coconut milk
- 1 cup crushed tomatoes
- 1/2 cup Greek yogurt
- 1 can (14oz) kidney beans, drained
- 1 tsp garlic
- 1 tsp paprika
- 1 tsp onion powder
- 1 tbsp butter
- Salt and pepper

Instructions:

In a pot, melt the butter, and fry the minced chicken.

Toss for 3 minutes. Add the jalapeno, and crushed tomatoes and cook for 5 minutes.

Add the garlic, paprika, salt, pepper, onion, and taco seasoning.

Cook for 5 minutes. Pour in water and cook for 20 minutes.

Add the coconut milk, and beans, and cook for 10 minutes.

Add the cheddar and cook for 10 minutes.

Serve hot with Greek yogurt on top.

7. Spicy Vegetarian Taco Soup

The delicious vegetarian-style taco soup is so amazing. The spice level is very high here, so If you enjoy the spices, then try this recipe.

Preparation Time: 10 minutes

Cooking Time: 1 hour

Serves: 4

Ingredients:

- 1 cup sliced mushrooms
- 1/2 cup corn kernels
- 1/2 cup crushed tomatoes
- 2 tbsp tamarind pulp
- 4 cups vegetable broth
- 2 tbsp honey
- 1/2 can (8 oz) kidney beans, drained
- 1 tsp garlic
- 1 tsp paprika
- 1 tbsp taco seasoning
- 1 tsp red chili powder
- 1 tsp oregano
- 1 tbsp cilantro, chopped
- 4 tsp Greek yogurt
- Salt and pepper

Instructions:

In a pot, add the vegetarian broth, with beans, and add the crushed tomatoes.

Add the spices, herbs, and seasoning.

Cook for 30 minutes. Add the mushrooms, tamarind pulp, and corn kernels, and cook for 10 minutes.

Add honey and cook for 4 minutes.

Serve with cilantro and Greek yogurt.

8. Shredded Chicken Taco Soup

This is a delicious taco soup recipe with shredded chicken. The tortilla chips on top add more flavor to the recipe.

Preparation Time: 10 minutes

Cooking Time: 2 hours

Serves: 6

Ingredients:

- 4 chicken breasts
- 1 cup corn kernels
- 1 tsp garlic
- 1 can (14oz) kidney beans, drained
- 6 cups water
- 1 tsp onion powder
- 1 cup crushed tomatoes
- 1 tsp paprika
- 2 tbsp taco seasoning
- Tortilla chips to serve
- 2 tbsp scallions, chopped
- 2 tomatoes, chopped
- Salt and pepper

Instructions:

In a large pot, add the chicken breasts with water.

Cover and cook for 30 minutes. Take the chicken out and shred it finely.

Add the crushed tomatoes, beans, spices, herbs, and seasoning.

Cook for 20 minutes. Return the chicken.

Add the corn and tomatoes and cook for 20 minutes.

Take off the heat. Serve hot with scallions, and tortilla chips on top.

9. Thick Beef Taco Soup

In this soup recipe, the broth is kind of thick and not runny. If you enjoy a bit different style then you must try this recipe.

Preparation Time: 5 minutes

Cooking Time: 1 hour

Serves: 4

Ingredients:

- 1 cup minced beef
- 3 cups water
- 1/2 cup corn kernels
- 1/2 cup crushed tomatoes
- 2 white onions, chopped
- 1 tbsp olive oil
- 1 can (14oz) kidney beans, drained
- 2 tomatoes, chopped
- 1 tsp garlic
- 1 tsp rosemary
- 1 tsp red chili powder
- 2 tbsp taco seasoning
- Salt and pepper

Instructions:

In a pot, heat the olive oil. Fry the beef for 5 minutes.

Add the onion, crushed tomatoes, beans and cook for 5 minutes.

Add spices, and seasoning and cook for 5 minutes.

Pour the water. Cook for 30 minutes.

Add the corn, and tomatoes. Cook for 15 minutes. Serve hot.

10. Zesty Lamb Taco Soup

The delicious creamy soup recipe is zesty, spicy, and a little bit sweet from the coconut milk.

Adding the avocado cubes is amazing.

Preparation Time: 5 minutes

Cooking Time: 2 hours

Serves: 6

Ingredients:

- 1 cup lamb, boneless, cut into small cubes
- 1 avocado, cubed
- 1 lime, cut into lemon wedges
- 2 tbsp cilantro, chopped
- 2 tbsp Green yogurt
- 4 tbsp cheddar cheese, grated
- 4 cups lamb broth
- 2 cups coconut milk
- 1 cup corn kernels
- 1 can (14oz) kidney beans
- 4 tomatoes, chopped, divided
- 1 tsp garlic
- 2 tbsp butter
- 1 tsp paprika
- 2 tbsp taco seasoning
- Salt and pepper

Instructions:

In a large pot, melt the butter and fry the lamb for 3 minutes.

Pour in the lamb broth and cook for 1 hour.

Add the garlic, salt, taco seasoning, pepper, and paprika.

Add half of the tomatoes and cook for 20 minutes.

Pour in the coconut milk, corn kernels, and beans.

Cook for 30 minutes. Take off the heat.

Serve with Greek yogurt, remaining tomatoes, avocado, cheese, lime slices, and cilantro on top.

11. Beef Gravy Taco Soup

Taco soup itself tastes great but adding beef gravy to it takes the taste to another level.

Preparation Time: 10 minutes

Cooking Time: 1 hour

Serves: 6

Ingredients:

- 1 cup beef gravy
- 4 cup water
- 1 cup minced beef
- 1 cup corn kernels
- 1 can (14oz) navy beans
- 1 cup chopped tomatoes
- 1 tsp garlic
- 1 tsp red chili powder
- 1 tsp pepper
- 2 tbsp taco seasoning
- Salt to taste
- Sour cream to serve
- Parsley, to serve
- Cheese to serve
- Chips to serve

Instructions:

In a pot, add the beef and stir for 2 minutes. Pour in the water.

Add salt, pepper, garlic, red chili powder, and taco seasoning.

Cook for 20 minutes. Add the beef gravy, beans, and tomatoes, and cook for 30 minutes.

Serve with parsley, cheese, chips, and sour cream.

12. Shredded Chicken Jalapeno Taco Soup

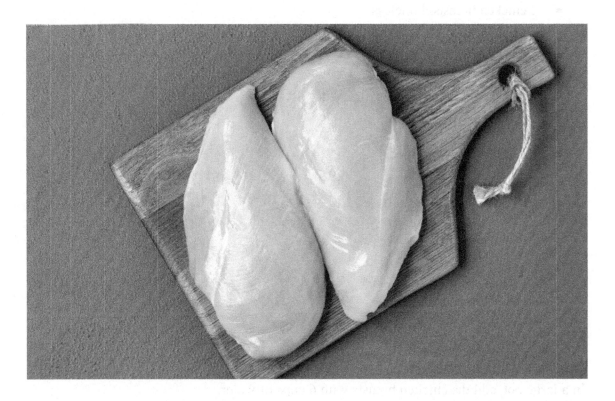

The shredded chicken with lima beans, black beans, and jalapeno is the perfect combination of a great taco soup.

Preparation Time: 5 minutes

Cooking Time: 1 hour

Serves: 6

Ingredients:

- 2 chicken breasts, boneless
- 1 can (14 oz) lima beans, drained
- 1 cup corn kernels
- 1 can (14oz) kidney beans, drained
- 4 tomatoes, chopped
- 1 cup jalapeno, chopped
- 2 tsp garlic
- 2 tsp paprika
- 3 tbsp taco seasoning
- Salt and pepper
- 2 tbsp parsley, chopped

Instructions:

In a large pot, add the chicken breasts with 6 cups of water.

Cook with the lid on for 30 minutes.

Take the chicken out and shred it finely.

Add the beans, jalapeno, tomatoes, spices, and seasoning.

Cook for 20 minutes. Add the shredded chicken, and corn and cook for 10 minutes.

Add parsley and serve hot.

13. Jalapeno Lamb Garlic Taco Soup

In this taco soup recipe, the flavor of garlic is very evident. The jalapeno in it also adds more texture to the recipe.

Preparation Time: 5 minutes

Cooking Time: 2 hours

Serves: 8

Ingredients:

- 2 cups minced lamb
- 1 cup corn kernels
- 6 tbsp cheddar cheese, grated
- 2 cups jalapeno, chopped
- 2 cups crushed tomatoes
- 4 tbsp parsley, chopped
- Greek yogurt to serve
- 2 can (28oz) kidney beans, drained
- 6 tomatoes, chopped
- 1 tsp garlic
- 1 tsp paprika
- 2 tbsp oil
- 2 tbsp taco seasoning
- Salt and pepper

Instructions:

In a pot, add the oil and fry the lamb for 5 minutes.

Pour in 6 cups of water and cook for 1 hour.

Add the spices, seasoning, beans, crushed tomatoes, and jalapeno.

Cook for 40 minutes. Add the corn, and tomatoes and cook for 10 minutes.

Take off the heat.

Add cheese, yogurt, parsley, and jalapeno on top. Serve.

14. Thick Vegetarian Taco Soup

This is a vegetarian taco soup with lima beans, kidney beans, and mushrooms.

Preparation Time: 10 minutes

Cooking Time: 30 minutes

Serves: 4

Ingredients:

- 1 cup mushrooms, sliced
- 1/2 cup corn kernels
- 1/2 cup crushed tomatoes
- 1 can (14oz) kidney beans
- 1 can (14oz) lima beans
- 2 tbsp taco seasoning
- 4 tbsp scallions, chopped
- 2 tbsp cheese, grated
- 1 tsp garlic
- 1 tsp oil
- 1 tsp paprika
- Salt and pepper

Instructions:

In a pot, add the oil and fry the mushrooms for 1 minute.

Drain the beans. Add to the pot.

Add the seasoning and spices.

Add the crushed tomatoes.

Add 2 cups of water. Cook for 15 minutes.

Add the corn and cook for 10 minutes.

Serve hot with cheese and scallions on top.

15. Vegetarian Kidney Bean Taco Soup

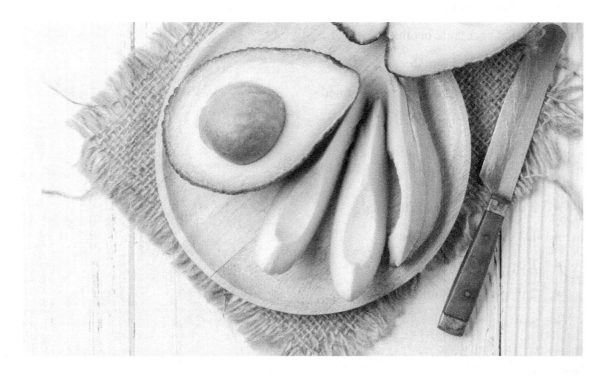

Here is another vegetarian taco soup with simple ingredients like kidney beans, tomatoes, corn, and avocado. Add a little feta cheese on top and it will taste better.

Preparation Time: 5 minutes

Cooking Time: 30 minutes

Serves: 4

Ingredients:

- 1/2 cup corn kernels
- 2 cups vegetable broth
- 1 cup crushed tomatoes
- 1 can (14oz) kidney beans, drained
- 2 tomatoes, chopped
- 1 tsp garlic
- 1 tsp onion powder
- 2 tbsp feta cheese, crumbled
- 1/3 cup avocado, cubes
- 1 tsp paprika
- 2 tbsp taco seasoning
- Salt and pepper

Instructions:

In a pot, add the beans with vegetable broth.

Cook for 10 minutes. Add the salt, pepper, taco, seasoning, paprika, onion, and garlic.

Cook for 2 minutes. Add tomatoes, crushed tomatoes, and corn.

Cook for 15 minutes. Serve hot with feta cheese, and avocado cubes on top.

16. Squash Carrot Kidney Bean Taco Soup

This delicious vegetarian taco soup is amazing with carrots, kidney beans, and squash.

Preparation Time: 10 minutes

Cooking Time: 40 minutes

Serves: 6

Ingredients:

- 1 cup carrot, chopped
- 1 cup corn kernels
- 1 cup crushed tomatoes
- 1 cup squash, cut into small cubes
- 1 tsp rosemary
- 1 can (14oz) kidney beans, drained
- 4 tomatoes, chopped
- 1 tsp garlic
- 1 tsp paprika
- 4 tbsp taco seasoning
- 1 tsp onion powder
- 1 tbsp oil
- Salt and pepper
- Avocado slices to serve
- Coriander to serve
- Sour cream to serve

Instructions:

In a large pot, add the oil.

Fry the squash and carrot.

Add spices, seasoning and herbs.

Cook for 5 minutes. Pour in 4 cups of water.

Cook for 20 minutes. Add the beans, crushed tomatoes, and tomatoes.

Add the corn kernels and cook for 15 minutes.

Serve with sour cream, coriander, and avocado.

17. Zesty Mutton Taco Soup

Minced mutton with corn, kidney beans, tomatoes, lemon and a strong flavor of ginger is evident in this taco soup.

Preparation Time: 5 minutes

Cooking Time: 1 hour

Serves: 6

Ingredients:

- 1 cup minced mutton
- 1 lemon, sliced
- 2 tbsp cilantro, chopped
- 1 cup corn kernels
- 2 cups crushed tomatoes
- 2 cans (28oz) kidney beans
- 1 tsp garlic
- 1 tbsp oil
- 1 tsp rosemary
- 1 tsp paprika
- 1 tsp ginger
- Sour cream to serve
- Tortilla chips to serve
- 3 tbsp taco seasoning
- Salt and pepper

Instructions:

In a large pot, heat the oil and fry the minced mutton for 5 minutes.

Drain the beans. Pour in 5 cups of water.

Cook for 30 minutes. Add the crushed tomatoes, corn, spices, and seasoning and cook for 25 minutes.

Take off the heat. Add lemon slices, sour cream, tortilla chips, and cilantro and serve hot.

18. Creamy and Cheesy Bean Taco Soup

This recipe is very thick in texture and full of flavors. You do not need to add any meat, so it will prepare quickly.

Preparation Time: 10 minutes

Cooking Time: 30 minutes

Serves: 4

Ingredients:

- 1/2 cup corn kernels
- 1/2 cup crushed tomatoes
- 1/2 can (8oz) lima beans
- 1 can (14oz) kidney beans
- 2 tomatoes, chopped
- 1/2 cup jalapeno, sliced
- 1 cup cheddar cheese, grated, divided
- Tortilla chips to serve
- 1 tsp garlic
- 1 tsp onion powder
- 1 cup heavy cream
- 2 tbsp taco seasoning
- Salt and pepper

Instructions:

Drain the beans.

Add to a pot. Pour in 4 cups of vegetable broth.

Cook for 10 minutes. Add spices, seasoning, crushed tomatoes, corn, tomatoes, jalapeno, and cook for 10 minutes.

Add the heavy cream and cook for 5 minutes.

Serve with tortilla chips, jalapenos, and cheese on top.

19. Lentil Jalapeno Taco Soup

This is a delicious vegetarian taco soup recipe that tastes very close to the non-vegetarian ones because of the lentils and the spices.

Preparation Time: 5 minutes

Cooking Time: 40 minutes

Serves: 6

Ingredients:

- 1 cup lentils
- 1 cup corn kernels
- 2 cups jalapeno, sliced
- 1 1/2 cups crushed tomatoes
- 1 can (14oz) kidney beans
- 2 tbsp parsley, chopped
- Sour cream to serve
- 1 tsp cumin
- 1 tsp garlic
- 1 tsp onion powder
- 1 tsp paprika
- 1 tsp oregano
- 5 cups vegetable broth
- 2 tbsp taco seasoning
- Salt and pepper

Instructions:

In a large pot, add the lentils with the vegetable broth.

Cook for 10 minutes.

Drain the beans and add to the pot.

Add the spices, seasoning, and crushed tomatoes, and cook for 10 minutes.

Add the corn and jalapeno.

Cook for 15 minutes. Serve hot with sour cream and parsley.

20. Pasta Taco Soup

You will be surprised to see how delicious pasta taco soup can be! The beans, the crushed tomatoes, cheese and sour cream, everything complements the pasta in the soup.

Preparation Time: 10 minutes

Cooking Time: 30 minutes

Serves: 6

Ingredients:

- 1 cup mushrooms, sliced
- 2 cups pasta
- 1 cup corn kernels
- 1 can (14oz) kidney beans
- 4 tbsp taco seasoning
- 1 tsp garlic
- 1 tbsp butter
- 1 cup crushed tomatoes
- 2 tsp paprika
- 1 tsp ginger
- Salt and pepper
- Parsley, chopped, to serve
- Sour cream, to serve

Instructions:

In a large pot, melt the butter and fry the mushroom for 1 minute.

Drain the beans and add to the pot.

Pour in 4 cups of vegetable broth.

Cook for 15 minutes. Add all the spices and seasoning.

Add the crushed tomatoes, corn, and pasta.

Cook for 10 minutes. Serve with parsley and sour cream.

21. Quinoa Taco Soup

The presence of quinoa in this taco soup makes it a wholesome lunch or dinner dish.

Preparation Time: 5 minutes

Cooking Time: 1 hour

Serves: 6

Ingredients:

- 1 can (14oz) kidney beans, drained
- 1 cup quinoa
- 1 cup corn kernels
- 4 tbsp taco seasoning
- 1 cup crushed tomatoes
- 1 cup minced beef
- 1 tsp garlic
- 1 tsp paprika
- 1 tsp onion powder
- 1 tbsp oil
- 1 lime, sliced
- 1/2 cup tortilla chips, to serve
- Avocado cubes, to serve
- Cilantro, chopped, to serve
- Salt and pepper

Instructions:

In a large pot, heat the oil over medium heat.

Fry the minced beef for 5 minutes.

Pour in 4 cups of water and cook for 30 minutes.

Add the crushed tomatoes, beans, spices, seasoning, and quinoa.

Cook for 20 minutes. Add the corn and cook for 10 minutes.

Serve hot with lime slices, tortilla chips, avocado and cilantro.

22. Chicken and Squash Taco Soup

The combination of chicken and squash in taco soup is quite good. The beans and corn in the soup are also an added plus to enhance the final flavor of the soup.

Preparation Time: 5 minutes

Cooking Time: 40 minutes

Serves: 6

Ingredients:

- 1 cup minced chicken
- 1 cup squash, cut into cubes
- 2 tbsp mint leaves
- 1 cup corn kernels
- 1 can (14oz) kidney beans
- 1 tbsp butter
- 1 cup crushed tomatoes
- 1 tsp garlic
- 1 tsp rosemary
- 1 tsp onion powder
- 1 tsp red chili powder
- 3 tbsp taco seasoning
- Salt and pepper

Instructions:

In a pot, melt the butter and fry the minced chicken for 4 minutes.

Pour in 4 cups of water. Cook for 10 minutes.

Add the crushed tomatoes, spices, and seasoning.

Cook for 10 minutes.

Add the beans, squash, and corn.

Cook for 10 minutes. Serve hot with mint leaves and sour cream.

23. Pork Taco Soup

This pork soup recipe is very simple yet has a massive flavor profile.

Preparation Time: 10 minutes

Cooking Time: 1 hour

Serves: 6

Ingredients:

- 1 cup minced pork
- 1 cup corn kernels
- 1 cup crushed tomatoes
- 1 cup heavy cream
- 1 tsp ginger powder
- 2 onion, chopped
- 4 cups water
- 1 tbsp butter
- 4 tomatoes, chopped
- 1 tsp garlic
- 1 tsp paprika
- 4 tbsp taco seasoning
- Salt and pepper
- Sour cream to serve
- Avocado slices to serve
- Cilantro, to serve

Instructions:

Melt the butter in a pot and fry the pork for 5 minutes.

Add 4 cups of water and cook for 1 hour.

Add the crushed tomato, seasoning, and spices, and cook for 20 minutes.

Add the corn, heavy cream and tomatoes.

Cook for 30 minutes. Serve hot with sour cream, avocado slices and cilantro.

24. Beef Tangy Taco Soup

The tanginess of the recipe is amazing. The beef cubes and squash in the recipe is amazing.

Preparation Time: 10 minutes

Cooking Time: 2 hours

Serves: 6

Ingredients:

- 2 cups beef, boneless, cut into cubes
- 2 cups squash, cut into cubes
- 1 tbsp tamarind pulp
- 1 cup crushed tomatoes
- 1 tsp garlic
- 1 tsp ginger
- 1 tsp paprika
- 1 tbsp oil
- 4 tbsp taco seasoning
- Salt and pepper
- Parsley, to serve
- Sour cream to serve

Instructions:

In a pot, heat the oil and fry the beef cubes for 5 minutes.

Pour in 4 cups of water.

Cook for 1 hour. Add ginger, garlic, paprika, taco seasoning, salt, and pepper.

Add crushed tomatoes and cook for 30 minutes.

Add the squash, and tamarind pulp and cook for 20 minutes.

Serve hot with parsley and sour cream.

25. Lamb Jalapeno Zesty Taco Soup

The delicious lamb chunks in the soup are amazing. The jalapeno in the recipe adds amazing texture to the soup.

Preparation Time: 10 minutes

Cooking Time: 4 hours

Serves: 8

Ingredients:

- 2 lb. Lamb, boneless, cut into small chunks
- 2 cups jalapeno, chopped
- 2 cups crushed tomatoes
- 2 cans (28oz) kidney beans
- 3 cups tomatoes, chopped
- 3 tsp garlic
- 3 tsp onion powder
- 3 tsp paprika
- 2 tbsp butter
- 5 tbsp taco seasoning
- Salt and pepper
- 2 tbsp parsley, chopped
- 1 lemon, cut into wedges

Instructions:

In a pot, melt the butter.

Fry the lamb and cook for 5 minutes.

Pour in 8 cups of water.

Cook for 2 hours. Add crushed tomatoes, tomatoes, beans, seasoning, and spices and cook for 1 hour.

Add the jalapeno and cook for 30 minutes.

Serve hot with lemon wedges.

26. Mushroom Vegetable Taco Soup

This taco soup is filled with vegetables which means It is more healthy and it has an abundance of flavor as well.

Preparation Time: 10 minutes

Cooking Time: 40 minutes

Serves: 6

Ingredients:

- 1 cup mushrooms, sliced
- 1 can (14oz) chickpeas, drained
- 1 cup corn kernels
- 1 cup crushed tomatoes
- 1 can (14oz) kidney beans, drained
- 4 tomatoes, chopped
- 1 cup carrots, chopped
- 1 cup squash, chopped
- 1 tsp garlic
- 1 tsp onion powder
- 1 tsp paprika
- 4 tbsp taco seasoning
- 2 tbsp mint, chopped
- Sour cream to serve
- Salt and pepper

Instructions:

In a large pot, add the crushed tomatoes with 4 cups of water.

Cook for 10 minutes.

Add the beans, mushrooms, spices, carrot, squash and seasoning.

Cook for 20 minutes. Add the tomatoes, and corn, and cook for 10 minutes.

Serve with mint leaves and sour cream on top.

27. Lamb Kidney Bean Taco Soup

This soup is slightly different as it does not uses tomatoes, which is one of the key elements of a taco soup. Yet, you will find this recipe refreshing and unique.

Preparation Time: 5 minutes

Cooking Time: 2 hours

Serves: 6

Ingredients:

- 1 cup minced lamb
- 1 cup corn kernels
- 1 cup lamb gravy
- 1 can (14oz) kidney beans, drained
- 1 cup jalapeno, chopped
- 1 tsp garlic
- 1 tsp ginger
- 1 tsp onion powder
- 1 tsp paprika
- 1 tsp cumin
- 4 tbsp taco seasoning
- Salt and pepper
- 1 tbsp butter
- Sour cream to serve
- Tortilla chips to serve
- Parsley, chopped, to serve

Instructions:

In a pot, melt the butter over medium heat.

Add the lamb and toss for 5 minutes.

Pour in 4 cups of water. Cook for 40 minutes.

Add the beans, jalapeno, and lamb gravy and cook for 30 minutes.

Add the spices, seasoning, and corn.

Cook for 20 minutes. Serve with parsley, tortilla chip, and sour cream.

28. Thick Onion Chicken Taco Soup

This soup is very thick and has an abundance of onion in it. If you enjoy thick soups then you will love this recipe.

Preparation Time: 5 minutes

Cooking Time: 1 hour

Serves: 6

Ingredients:

- 1 cup minced chicken
- 1 cup onion, chopped
- 1 cup heavy cream
- 1 cup corn kernels
- 1 cup crushed tomatoes
- 1 can (14oz) kidney beans
- 1 tsp garlic
- 1 tsp paprika
- 4 tbsp taco seasoning
- 1 tbsp oil
- Salt and pepper
- Tortilla chips to serve

Instructions:

In a large pot, add the oil over medium heat.

Add the chicken and cook for 5 minutes.

Pour in 4 cups of water and cook for 20 minutes.

Add the crushed tomatoes, spices, and seasoning.

Cook for 10 minutes. Add corn, onion, heavy cream, and beans.

Cook for 20 minutes. Serve with tortilla chips on top.

29. Shredded Chicken Kidney Bean Taco Soup

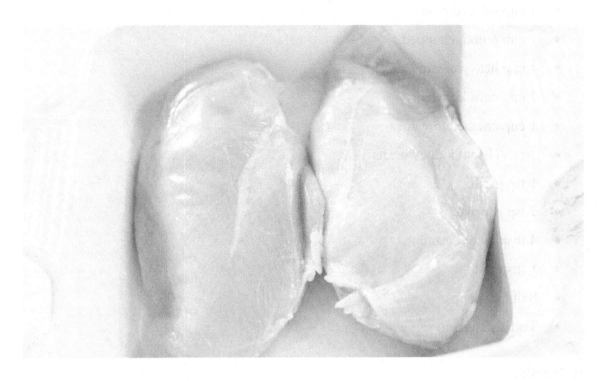

This is a kind of clear taco soup with shredded chicken in it. The red bell pepper in it adds a different texture to the soup.

Preparation Time: 4 minutes

Cooking Time: 1 hour

Serves: 8

Ingredients:

- 4 chicken breasts, boneless
- 2 red bell pepper, cut into medium chunks
- 2 cans (28oz) black beans, drained
- 1 tsp garlic
- 1 tsp onion powder
- 1 tsp paprika
- 5 tbsp taco seasoning
- 6 cups chicken broth
- Salt and pepper
- Sour cream to serve

Instructions:

In a large pot, add the chicken with chicken broth.

Cover and cook for 30 minutes.

Take the chicken out and shred it finely.

Add spices and seasoning to the pot.

Add beans, and bell pepper. Cook for 10 minutes.

Return the shredded chicken to the pot.

Cook for 20 minutes. Serve with sour cream on top.

30. Spicy Shredded Beef Taco Soup

This taco soup with shredded beef in it is rather spicy. If you enjoy the spices then you will fall in love with this one-of-a-kind taco soup.

Preparation Time: 10 minutes

Cooking Time: 4 hours

Serves: 6

Ingredients:

- 1 cup beef chunks, boneless
- 1 cup brown gravy
- 2 can (28oz) kidney beans, drained
- 1 tsp garlic
- 1 tsp oregano
- 1 cup jalapeno, sliced
- 1 tsp onion powder
- 1 tsp paprika
- 1 tsp cumin
- 4 tbsp taco seasoning
- Salt and pepper
- Avocado cubes to serve
- Yogurt to serve
- Tortilla chips to serve

Instructions:

In a pot, add the beef chunks with 8 cups of water.

Cover and cook for 2 hours.

Take the beef out and shred them finely.

Add the spices and seasoning to the pot. Add jalapeno, beans, and brown gravy.

Cook for 40 minutes. Return the shredded beef.

Cook for 1 hour. Serve with yogurt, tortilla chips, and avocado cubes.

Conclusion

Taco soup is something that not only the Mexican origin love but people around the world adore the massive flavor of this recipe. The good thing is it is not just one recipe, it comes with a wide variety of recipes. The base is simple, yet you cannot get enough of it because of how flavorful it really is! These taco soup recipes are suitable for an evening with special guests, at the same time, you can choose a simple recipe that is suitable for lazy noon too. You can make a big batch if you live alone and enjoy it for a week if properly refrigerated. In the book, the 30 taco soup recipes are fun and flavorful, and some of them are rather quick. Some of them do require hours to make because the meat needs to be tender to get the maximum flavor out of it. But you can also choose to make it vegetarian and make it in under 1 hour too. Try the recipes and see which one stands out in your book.

Author's Afterthoughts

Lately, I've been trying to come up with ideas for my new cookbooks, but I thought that your ideas could be a huge help. Sure, I develop the recipes, but you're the one who makes them at home and brings them into your life! As a result, I want my recipes to be filled with flavors and ingredients that you keep in your kitchen at all times, ready to surprise unexpected guests.

I know a lot of my books are centered around treats and dishes for special occasions, but what else would you like to see from me? I'm still working on outlines, so now's the time to share your input with me. Do you think they are easy enough to follow along? Are the ingredients generally easy to find in your local supermarket? Would you like to see more recipes oriented toward a certain cuisine?

The only reason I have this amazing job and cook delicious food for a living is because of you, so now it's my turn to say thanks and contribute to your menus by preparing a cookbook worthy of your kitchen.

Thanks a bunch, xxx

Jayden Dixon

About the Author

How Jayden stumbled into the kitchen after spending much of her life working in oil rigs around the world is something she's not quite able to herself, but everyone is equally excited that she did! Working in some of the most remote locations on earth, literally cut off from civilization, she admits cooking (or eating) wasn't her favorite thing to do. Ingredients were pretty limited, as were food storage options with many people on the platform.

Whenever she video called friends and family, she liked to joke that canned tuna was her favorite meal! Fortunately, when her job permanently relocated her to actual land, she fell in love with supermarkets. Her mom says that's the only place Jayden went to and spent hours in for the first three months. Funnily enough, Jayden also happened to meet her husband, Max, at the supermarket, right by the canned goods aisle!

Neither of them knew how to cook, but they kept at it until they became amateur cooks capable of exceptional dishes. Word of mouth spread little by little, and locals started asking the pair to cater to their events. Eventually, the cooking began to eat up too much of their schedules, and they decided to quit their jobs and start their catering business in Milwaukee, Wisconsin. Six years later, Jayden and Max run the biggest catering service in Wisconsin. They have 3 lovely kids and 5 fluffy cats.

Made in the USA
Monee, IL
12 November 2023

46364558R00044